Holy-ish: A Relatable Guide to Healing and Self Discovery

Dedication

To London and Mars, my entire world. May you grow in faith, courage, and self-love, knowing you are deeply cherished.

Table of Contents

Introduction: So… You're a Hot Mess

Let's be real: life feels like trying to fold a fitted sheet, confusing, humbling, and slightly embarrassing when you realize everyone else is just winging it too. You thought by now you'd have it all together, emotionally healed, spiritually aligned, financially stable, skin glowing from within. Instead, some days you're like, God, it's me again… spiraling."

Welcome to healing.

This book isn't about pretending everything's perfect. It's about finding peace in the process, learning how to laugh through the mess, cry when you need to, pray when you can, and give yourself grace on the days you forget how to do all three.

I wrote this for the person who's tired of acting like healing has a timeline. For the one balancing faith and therapy, brunch and Bible study, boundaries and burnout. For the woman who loves Jesus but also has questions, side-eyes, and a therapist on speed dial.

We're going to talk about trauma, the kind we grew up with and the kind we accidentally recreate. We'll talk about faith, therapy, friendships, purpose, and that awkward in-between space where you're becoming but still a little broken.

And yes, we'll laugh. Because healing is serious work, but God didn't call us to be miserable while we do it. Joy is holy too.

You don't need to have it all figured out. You just need a willing heart, a sense of humor, and maybe a good candle.

So, take a deep breath. Grab your notebook, your tea (or your wine, no judgment), and let's start this journey together. Healing isn't about being perfect, it's about becoming whole.

Chapter 1: The Trauma We Don't Post About

We all have that "one thing" we swore we were over until something small reminds us that… nope, still healing. Maybe it's that one song that hits too hard, that one conversation that leaves your chest tight, or that one person who pops up and suddenly you're questioning every boundary you've ever set.

That's the thing about trauma. It doesn't always look like crying in a corner. Sometimes it looks like overworking yourself because rest feels unsafe. Sometimes it looks like being the strong friend because you never learned how to be cared for. Sometimes it looks like laughing everything off so you don't have to admit it still hurts.

We don't post this part online. We post the glow-up, not the growing pains. We post the healed version, not the healing process. But healing doesn't happen in public; it happens in the quiet moments when you finally stop pretending you're fine and start telling yourself the truth.

I had to learn that my trauma wasn't just what happened to me, it was also what I learned to do to survive. The people-pleasing, the perfectionism, the "I got it" attitude, all of it was a shield. But you can't grow behind a shield; eventually, you have to put it down.

Healing means letting God into the places you've been trying to protect. It's realizing He already knows what broke you, and He still calls you whole. It's messy, uncomfortable, and sometimes you'll want to quit. But every time you choose honesty over denial, grace over guilt, you're taking a step toward freedom.

You don't need to have a deep childhood revelation to start healing. You just need awareness, that gentle, uncomfortable realization that something inside you deserves attention. Start there. Ask yourself, what am I still carrying that I thought I left behind?

Healing begins when you stop running from that question and start sitting with it.

And before you roll your eyes, no, this doesn't mean you have to relive every painful memory. It just means you start being honest about how those memories shaped you. The truth might sting, but it's never meant to shame you, it's meant to set you free.

So here's your challenge for this week: Sit with yourself. Not your phone, not your to-do list, but yourself. Ask God to reveal what's hiding beneath the surface. Journal it, pray about it, laugh at it if you need to. But don't ignore it.

Because the things we don't post about are usually the very things God wants to heal first.

Soul Work

1. What's something you've been pretending doesn't bother you anymore?
2. How does your body react when you feel triggered or uncomfortable? (tight chest, avoidance, overexplaining, shutting down?)
3. What survival habits might you still be holding on to that no longer serve you?
4. When was the last time you were completely honest with God about how you feel?
5. Write a short prayer or affirmation releasing one piece of pain you've been carrying.

Chapter 2: Purpose, Delays, and Divine Timing

When life doesn't go how you planned, it's easy to feel frustrated, impatient, or even like you've failed. But delays aren't denials. They're part of God's timing, teaching patience, refining character, and preparing you for what's next. Trusting God's "not yet" means embracing the in-between seasons without losing hope. It's showing up faithfully in the work you can do now, even if the bigger vision hasn't arrived yet. It's learning that growth often happens behind the scenes, in moments no one sees, when no milestone has been checked off. Finding your calling in the in-between requires self-reflection, openness, and faith. Ask yourself what lights your soul on fire, what serves others, and how your gifts can be used even before the dream is fully realized. The journey is just as sacred as the destination. Delays don't mean you're forgotten or that your dreams aren't valid. They mean God is shaping your timing, aligning opportunities, and preparing your heart. Trust the process, continue showing up, and lean into the lessons that only patience can teach.

Soul Work

1. Reflect on a delay or detour in your life and how it has shaped your growth.
2. Identify one way you can use your current season to move closer to your calling.
3. Pray or journal about trusting God's timing even when it doesn't match your plan.
4. List three lessons you've learned from past "not yet" moments.
5. Write a short affirmation reminding yourself that your timing is in God's hands.

Chapter 3: Letting Go Without Losing Yourself

Letting go is hard. Sometimes it feels like your heart is holding a suitcase full of memories, regrets, and "what ifs" that you are not ready to unpack. And then someone tells you to "just move on," and you are like, Excuse me, Karen, it's not that simple.

Letting go does not mean forgetting, excusing, or minimizing what happened. It does not mean pretending you are fine when you are not. Letting go is about releasing control over things you cannot change and trusting God to handle what is out of your hands. It is about freeing yourself from weight that is holding you back from peace, joy, and growth.

Practically, letting go might mean ending toxic relationships, forgiving someone who hurt you, or releasing expectations that no longer serve your purpose. It might mean changing your environment, setting firm boundaries, or simply deciding to stop revisiting the past in your mind.

The process is rarely linear. You will have days when you feel lighter and days when the old pain resurfaces. That is normal. Letting go takes patience, self-compassion, and persistence. It also requires leaning on God and trusting that His plan for your life is bigger than your current pain or disappointment.

Humor can help too. Laughing at your own drama, at how messy life can be, or even at your overthinking tendencies reminds you that letting go does not have to be solemn or heavy all the time. You can release with grace, with faith, and yes, with a little laughter along the way.

Remember, letting go is not about losing yourself. It is about reclaiming your energy, your peace, and your power. You are not abandoning your story. You are choosing to write the next chapter with intention, hope, and faith.

Soul Work

1. Identify one person, habit, or situation you need to let go of.
2. Reflect on why holding on has kept you stuck.
3. Write a prayer or journal entry releasing control and trusting God with the outcome.
4. List three ways letting go will positively impact your life and well-being.
5. Think of one small action you can take this week to begin the process of release.

Chapter 4: Self-Care Isn't Selfish (Even When You're Busy)

Let's be real. Life is chaotic. Work, family, side hustles, social obligations, and the constant scroll of social media can make self-care feel like a luxury you simply do not have time for. But here's the thing, self-care is not a luxury. It's a necessity. You cannot pour from an empty cup, and no one else can fill it for you.

Self-care looks different for everyone. It could be a 10-minute meditation in the morning, a long bath at night, a walk outside, or even just sitting quietly with your thoughts and a cup of coffee. It could be saying no to extra responsibilities that drain your energy. It could be setting healthy boundaries with people who consistently take more than they give.

Spiritual self-care is just as important. Prayer, reflection, journaling, or even reading a devotional can help you reconnect with God and your purpose. This is the fuel that keeps your spirit nourished, even on days when everything else feels overwhelming.

Physical and mental self-care go hand in hand. Exercise, rest, nutrition, and mindfulness are practical ways to care for your body and mind.

When you take the time to nurture yourself, you become more resilient, more patient, and more present in your relationships and responsibilities.

Self-care does not have to be complicated or expensive. It's the small, consistent actions that make the biggest difference. Give yourself permission to rest, reflect, and recharge without guilt.

Soul Work

1. List three small self-care actions you can do this week, no matter how busy you are.
2. Reflect on moments when you neglected your self-care and how it affected you.
3. Identify one boundary you can set to protect your energy and time.
4. Write a short prayer or journal entry reconnecting with your spirit and purpose.
5. Celebrate one moment this week where you prioritized yourself without guilt.

Chapter 5: Generational Curses

Generational curses are more than family folklore or church talk. They're the patterns we inherit, the pain we normalize, and the silence we mistake for strength. They show up in how we communicate, how we love, and how we protect ourselves.

Some of us were raised in homes where emotions were treated like secrets. You didn't cry, you "sucked it up." You didn't ask for help, you "figured it out." You didn't talk about what hurt, you just "moved on." But the truth is, what we don't heal, we hand down.

Healing generational wounds means telling the truth about what happened, what didn't, and how it shaped us. It means seeing your parents as people, not just authority figures. It means forgiving without pretending you weren't hurt. It means saying, "God, I love them, but I want better."

Sometimes the hardest part of healing family patterns is realizing you can't change anyone else. You can only change how you respond. You can't make your parents go to therapy, but you can stop repeating their pain. You can't force your family to understand boundaries, but you can honor yours.

When God heals you, He's not just healing your life, He's healing generations through you. You are the interruption your bloodline needed.

Every act of self-awareness, every prayer for patience, every time you choose peace over chaos, you are rewriting history. You are proof that the curse ends here.

Soul Work

1. Reflect on one pattern you've seen passed down in your family. How has it affected you?
2. What does "breaking a cycle" mean to you personally?
3. What's one boundary that helps protect your peace when dealing with family conflict?
4. How can you honor your family's story while still choosing a different path?
5. Write a short prayer asking God to help you heal what your family didn't know how to.

Chapter 6: Friendships, Boundaries, and the Art of the Soft No

Friendships are tricky. Sometimes they feel like a warm hug, and other times they feel like juggling flaming swords while someone is asking for a favor. You want to show up for the people you love, but you also need to show up for yourself. And that is where boundaries come in.

Boundaries are not punishment. They are not walls to keep people out. They are gates that protect your energy and allow you to show up fully when you are ready. Saying no does not make you a bad friend. It makes you a self-aware one. Learning the soft no, the polite, firm, non-guilty version, is a superpower. It might feel uncomfortable at first, but it is liberating.

Boundaries also teach people how to treat you. If you never say no, people assume you are endlessly available. If you always say yes, you teach others that your energy is not valuable. Boundaries are an act of self-respect and a reflection of how much you value your mental, emotional, and spiritual health.

Some practical ways to set boundaries include clearly defining your availability, limiting contact with people who drain you, and communicating your needs honestly. It is okay to skip that group text conversation, decline plans that feel exhausting, or step back from relationships that pull you down. Boundaries are not selfish. They are essential for thriving friendships and a healthy life.

Good friendships nourish you. They do not deplete you. They make space for laughter, vulnerability, and support without guilt or shame. The art of the soft no is learning that you can love deeply and fully without sacrificing your own well-being.

Soul Work

1. Identify one area in your friendships where you struggle to say no.
2. Reflect on how saying yes too often has affected your energy, emotions, or spiritual growth.
3. Practice one soft no this week in a way that protects your boundaries without creating guilt.
4. List the qualities you want in friendships that support your growth and healing.
5. Pray or journal about the friendships that help you show up as your best self.

Chapter 7: Faith Over Feelings (Even When You Don't Feel Like It)

Some days, faith feels effortless. You wake up, read a verse, pray, and the world seems a little lighter. Other days, you're staring at your ceiling at 2 a.m., wondering if God forgot your prayer or if He's just tired of your questions.

Here's the truth: faith isn't about how you feel in the moment. It's about choosing to trust God even when your emotions are messy. It's about saying yes to hope when your heart is screaming no. It's about leaning on Him when logic, fear, or hurt try to take the wheel.

I've learned that feelings are sneaky. They can tell you lies like, I'm alone, I'm not worthy, God doesn't see me. But God's truth doesn't change just because your feelings do. Faith is the bridge between your current reality and God's promises. Sometimes it's quiet. Sometimes it's messy. And sometimes it's downright hilarious when you realize you've been praying for wisdom while making every possible wrong decision anyway.

Choosing faith over feelings doesn't mean ignoring your emotions. It means bringing them to God honestly, letting Him hold them, and letting Him remind you that He's bigger than your current struggle. It's waking up, saying a small prayer, and trusting that God can handle what you can't.

Faith also grows through community. Talking with friends who share your beliefs, attending worship, reading scripture, or even just texting your prayer buddy. These small acts remind you that God's love isn't just theoretical. It's lived, experienced, and practical.

When you choose faith over feelings, you start to notice that God's timing is perfect, even when your heart is impatient. You begin to see doors opening that your anxiety never would have allowed you to notice. You start walking in peace, knowing that God's plans for you are bigger than what you can see right now.

Soul Work

1. Identify one area of your life where your feelings are making you doubt God's plan.
2. Write down what the truth says about that situation, based on scripture or spiritual insight.
3. How can you bring your emotions honestly to God without letting them control your decisions?
4. Name one small action you can take this week to choose faith over feelings.
5. Pray for the courage to trust God even when it doesn't feel easy.

Chapter 8: Jesus Take the Wheel and Therapy Bills

Ever notice how self-care isn't just bubble baths and smoothies, but also tough conversations, therapy sessions, and figuring out what actually works for you? Some days that looks like journaling your thoughts at 2 a.m., other days it looks like scheduling a session with a therapist or talking honestly with a friend about your feelings. Healing and personal growth aren't one-size-fits-all, and what works for one person might not work for you and that's okay.

Healing spiritually and emotionally doesn't have to be fancy, but it does require intentionality. Journaling is a perfect example. A simple notebook can be your confessional, your therapist, and your prayer closet all in one. You write down your fears, your frustrations, and yes, even the ridiculous thoughts you think you're "too grown" to have. You can cry on paper, laugh at your own dramatic tendencies, and then hand it all over to God.

Therapy is another piece of the puzzle. Some days it's about unpacking childhood trauma, other days it's about learning how to communicate like a normal adult without screaming or ghosting. And yes, it costs money but consider it an investment in the most important project: yourself. Remember, Jesus didn't say, "Blessed are the perfect," He said, "Blessed are the peacemakers," and that includes making peace within yourself.

Blending faith and therapy isn't contradictory. It's complementary. Journals, prayers, and therapy sessions all work together to help you process life, grow spiritually, and stop repeating patterns that no longer serve you.

Sometimes, you'll write a whole page of prayers and realize you've been praying for the wrong things. Sometimes, you'll leave therapy feeling like you still have ten miles to go. That's okay. Healing isn't a checklist; it's a journey. And God meets you at every step, whether it's through scripture, therapy, or a messy journal entry at 2 a.m.

At the end of the day, the goal isn't to have it all together. The goal is to show up, do the work, and trust God with the process. And if you can laugh a little along the way, even better.

Soul Work

1. Write down three things that are weighing on your heart right now. Offer them to God in prayer.
2. Choose one journal entry this week to reflect on honestly, including emotions you normally hide.
3. List one habit or behavior you want to work on in therapy or personal reflection.
4. Identify one small way to combine faith and personal growth in your daily routine.
5. Write a humorous or honest prayer thanking God for meeting you exactly where you are.

Chapter 9: Healing Isn't Pretty (But Neither Is Avoidance)

Healing is messy. There's no Instagram filter that makes crying in your car at 7 a.m. look inspirational. There's no cute TikTok dance that magically fixes the heartbreak, the anxiety, or the stress that shows up in your everyday life. And yet, we spend so much energy trying to make healing look neat, tidy, and impressive.

The truth is that avoidance might feel easier in the moment. Ignoring old wounds, sweeping feelings under the rug, and pretending everything is fine seems like a safe shortcut. But avoidance never frees you. It keeps you stuck, repeating patterns, and carrying burdens you don't need. Healing requires courage, the kind that lets you sit with discomfort and say, "I see you, I feel you, and I will walk through this with God."

Some days healing will feel slow. Other days it will feel like progress overnight. You might have moments where you want to quit, or where the pain feels too heavy to carry. That's okay. Messy healing is still healing. Imperfect steps toward growth are still steps. And leaning into God, even when you feel weak or uncertain, is always a victory.

Practical ways to navigate the mess include journaling your raw thoughts, naming your triggers without judgment, setting boundaries with people who drain you, and carving out space to rest. Healing is active. It's doing the hard work even when you don't feel like it and trusting God to meet you in the middle.

Remember, you don't have to have it all together to make progress. Sometimes progress looks like showing up anyway, crying anyway, forgiving anyway, and praying anyway. Healing isn't pretty but it's worth it.

Soul Work

1. Write down one thing you've been avoiding that's keeping you stuck.
2. Reflect on how avoidance has shown up in your life and what patterns it has reinforced.
3. What is one small step you can take this week toward facing that issue?
4. Pray or reflect on God's presence as you step into the uncomfortable.
5. List three ways you can show yourself grace while working through messy emotions.

Chapter 10: Joy Is Also Holy

Joy and laughter are not frivolous, they are sacred. Finding moments of joy while healing is an act of worship, a declaration that your heart is alive, grateful, and resilient. Creating joy doesn't mean ignoring pain. It means allowing yourself to celebrate the small wins, the funny moments, the beauty around you, even while working through struggles. It's dancing in your living room, laughing at a silly meme, calling a friend just to share a laugh, or savoring your favorite cup of coffee without guilt.

Joy is a practice. It's noticing the gifts in your everyday life, giving thanks for them, and sharing that joy with others. It replenishes your spirit, strengthens your faith, and reminds you that God delights in your happiness. Healing and growth are serious work, but joy reminds you that life is meant to be lived fully. Your laughter, your smiles, your celebration of life are acts of spiritual resistance against despair, exhaustion, and cynicism. They are holy because they honor the life God has given you, the journey you're on, and the love that surrounds you.

Soul Work

1. Identify three simple things that bring you genuine joy this week.
2. Reflect on a recent moment when you laughed or smiled authentically. What made it special?
3. Write a gratitude list focusing on joy-filled experiences or relationships.
4. Pray or journal about inviting more joy into your daily routine.
5. Be intentional this week to celebrate life, even in the midst of challenges.

Chapter 11: Main Character Energy Meets Humility

Let's be honest. Wanting to feel like the main character isn't inherently bad. You deserve to show up fully in your life, unapologetically, and claim your worth. The tricky part is doing it without tipping into ego or self-centeredness. That's where humility comes in.

Main character energy is about confidence rooted in God, not in external validation or social media clout. It's knowing your value comes from being His creation, not from likes, promotions, or someone else recognizing your greatness. True confidence doesn't need applause. It simply shows up, does its work, and shines quietly without stepping on anyone else's spotlight.

Showing up fully as yourself means leaning into your strengths while being honest about your weaknesses. It's celebrating wins without shaming others for theirs. It's saying "I see you" to others while saying "I see me" too. It's walking into a room knowing who you are, while keeping your ego in check and your heart open.

Practical ways to embody this balance include reflecting on your intentions. Before speaking, posting, or acting, ask yourself: "Am I showing up for God's glory or just for my own validation?" Celebrate small wins quietly. Gratitude journals, prayer, or acknowledging God in your achievements keeps humility at the center. Serve others. True main character energy includes lifting others up, mentoring, or simply listening. Humility isn't shrinking yourself. It's expanding your space for everyone. Stay self-aware. Ego sneaks in when we stop reflecting. Daily check-ins with yourself or with God help keep confidence healthy. Use your influence responsibly. Whether at work, in your friend group, or online, showing your gifts with kindness is main character energy done right.

Main character energy meets humility when you own your story while remembering God wrote the plot. You shine, you lead, you inspire, but you also stay grounded, kind, and aware that your journey is bigger than just you.

Confidence doesn't have to be loud. Sometimes it's the quiet courage to walk in your purpose, speak your truth, and love yourself and others well, all while keeping your ego on a leash.

Soul Work

1. Write down three ways you can show up confidently without letting ego take the wheel.
2. Reflect on a moment when your confidence felt rooted in God versus external validation.
3. Identify one area where humility could improve your relationships or self-perception.
4. Pray or journal about balancing ambition, main character energy, and kindness.
5. List one small action this week to celebrate yourself while uplifting someone else.

Chapter 12: Walking in Purpose Without Losing Your Mind

Stepping into your purpose can feel equal parts exciting and exhausting. Some days you are on fire, feeling like you can conquer the world. Other days you are staring at your to-do list wondering if you accidentally signed up for a lifetime of chaos disguised as destiny.

Purpose does not mean perfection. It does not mean having all the answers or never doubting yourself. Purpose is about showing up consistently, leaning into your gifts, and trusting God with the results. It is about taking steps, even small ones, toward what lights your soul on fire, while giving yourself grace for the missteps along the way.

One key to walking in purpose without losing your mind is clarity. Know your values, your strengths, and your non-negotiables. When you understand what matters most, it becomes easier to say no to distractions, to people, or to opportunities that do not align with your path. This protects your energy and keeps you focused on what really counts.

Another key is community. Purpose was never meant to be walked alone. Surround yourself with people who encourage, challenge, and support you. Seek mentorship, collaboration, and honest feedback. Let God use others to guide and lift you when your own strength falters.

Remember, balance does not mean doing everything perfectly. It means creating harmony between your calling, your well-being, and your relationships. It means giving yourself permission to rest, reflect, and recharge so that you can serve fully without burning out.

Most importantly, trust God. He designed you uniquely, equipped you with everything you need, and has a plan for your life that goes beyond what you can see right now. Walking in purpose is a journey, and faith is your compass. Lean into it, trust it, and let it guide you with peace and confidence.

Soul Work

1. Reflect on what makes you feel most alive and aligned with your purpose.
2. Write down three small steps you can take this week to move toward your calling.
3. Identify one area where you tend to overcommit or overthink and plan a way to simplify.
4. Journal or pray about trusting God with your next steps and the outcome.
5. List the people or resources you can lean on to support you as you walk in purpose.

Chapter 13: Becoming Him/Her (and Still Becoming)

If you've made it this far, congratulations. You're still here. You're still trying. And most importantly, you're still becoming. Healing is not a one-and-done moment. Faith is not a checklist. Self-love is not a destination. This chapter isn't about telling you you're "fixed" or "perfect." It's about celebrating the fact that you've kept going, even when it was messy, hard, and sometimes downright confusing.

Becoming is a lifelong process. Some days you'll feel like you've got it all together. Other days you'll feel like you're back at square one. Both are part of the journey. Both are valid. Both are proof that you are human, growing, and alive.

Look back for a moment. Think about where you started, the wounds you've carried, the prayers you've whispered, the boundaries you've learned to set, the tears you've shed, and the courage you've found. You are not the same person you were yesterday, last year, or even five years ago. You are evolving. You are becoming.

Faith, healing, and self-love are intertwined. As you lean into God, you learn patience with yourself. As you confront trauma and embrace your journey, you learn resilience. As you practice self-love, you find joy in the small moments, the quiet victories, and the laughter along the way. Each step forward, no matter how small, is progress.

Becoming is not about arriving. It's about showing up for yourself, for others, and for God. It's about trusting the process and giving yourself grace when you stumble. It's about noticing your growth and giving thanks for every lesson, every setback, and every breakthrough.

So take a moment to be grateful. Be grateful for how far you've come. Be grateful for the strength you didn't know you had. Be grateful for the love, guidance, and faith that have carried you here. And most importantly, be excited for the person you are still becoming.

You are a work in progress. A masterpiece in motion. A story still unfolding. And that is something worth celebrating every single day.

Soul Work

1. Reflect on three ways you've grown since you started your healing journey.
2. Write a gratitude list of people, experiences, or practices that have supported your growth.
3. Identify one area where you are still "becoming" and commit to showing up there this week.
4. Pray or journal about trusting God with the rest of your journey.
5. Write a short affirmation acknowledging your progress and embracing your ongoing growth.

Epilogue: Healing Out Loud and Doing the Work

Dear Reader,

If you're holding this book, that means you showed up. You turned the page. You dared to look at your own mess, your own heart, your own story and that's brave. And honestly, so am I. I'm still figuring it out too. Some days I feel like I've got it together, other days I'm Googling "how to adult" while crying over my bank statement. Healing is messy, awkward, and gloriously imperfect and guess what? That's exactly how it's supposed to be.

We're learning, stumbling, praying, laughing, and occasionally eating ice cream for breakfast because, why not? And in the middle of it all, God is showing up, gently reminding us that progress matters more than perfection. That joy is holy. That our stories, however tangled, are worth telling.

So, keep showing up. Keep loving yourself, questioning yourself, and trusting yourself enough to lean into the messy work of growth. Keep laughing, keep crying, and keep praying even if your prayers are just, "Help me not screw this up today."

We're healing out loud and doing the work together. And that, my friend, is a beautiful thing.

With all my love, gratitude, and a little bit of sass,
Brittany B. Alexander

www.ingramcontent.com/pod-product-compliance
Lightning Source LLC
Chambersburg PA
CBHW071950100426
42736CB00042B/2690